Abide.
Arise.
Ascend.

Jordyn M. Dunlap

Abide. Arise. Ascend

Abide. Arise. Ascend

Abide. Arise. Ascend
Copyright and Acknowledgements

Scripture translations:
KJV-King James Version

Edited for publication by Alicia C. Dunlap - WordSong Publishing

Cover design by Des'Za'Rae King and Jeremy Prader

Printing: Sterling Pierce, New York, NY

This book can be purchased by contacting:
AC Dunlap – acdunlap28@gmail.com or acdunlap.wordsong@gmail.com

Abide. Arise. Ascend

Dedication:

This book is dedicated to every beautiful soul drowning in the chaos of worldly affirmation. Who you are cannot be found in the fruitless things of this world, but in Jesus Christ alone. May these words empower you to pursue your identity in the love of the Father, and give you the courage to live boldly in your inheritance.

Abide. Arise. Ascend

About the Author:

Jordyn M. Dunlap is a native of Columbus, Ohio. Currently serving as an Anchor and Producer for ABC6 Columbus, she's been blessed to transition her career back to her hometown. Before landing her anchoring position with ABC6, she worked down the road for NBC4 Columbus.

Before joining the ranks as on-air talent, Jordyn was able to gain valuable experience within her career field. Over the years, she's acquired skills from internships with prominent news outlets such *as WBNS 10TV News, CNN, The New York Times*, and *ABC News* in West Perth Australia. Although she's

Abide. Arise. Ascend

learned so much over the years, she knows there is always room for growth.

"Working for NBC4 is one of my greatest blessings. As a journalist, serving as a voice for the voiceless in my community is what makes my heart come alive, and what better place to deliver quality, accurate news coverage than in the town I know all too well."

While Jordyn is passionate about news, her love for prayer is even greater. For two years, Jordyn helped to lead BURN 24/7 Columbus which is a global prayer and worship movement started by Bethel worship leader, Sean Feucht. Through intercession, missions work, and more, Burn 24/7 allots space for these things to be accomplished in an atmosphere of freedom. From 6 am to 8 am Monday through Thursday mornings, she led prayer meetings along with another member of the leadership team. She believes the BURN helped save her life and she's honored to grow in her walk with the Lord, in leadership, and ministry through BURN 24/7 Columbus.

In addition to her career in television news, Jordyn is the founder and C.E.O of iLive the Movement. Serving as a platform of support for

Abide. Arise. Ascend

survivors of any form of mental illness, Jordyn's non-profit has been impacting lives across the globe since 2017. The birthing of her business was launched through the overcoming of her own mental health struggles.

In December of 2016, Jordyn was rushed to the ER for a suicide attempt and hospitalized for a week in Dublin Springs Behavioral Hospital. Her suicide attempt stemmed from deep-rooted insecurities, relationship trauma, self-hatred, and identity confusion. Thankfully, God used this traumatic experience to alter the entire trajectory of her life, and she identifies the experience as "unforgettable."

Abide. Arise. Ascend

Table of Contents:

Abide. Arise. Ascend

Preface

Hi friends!

My name is Jordyn Dunlap and I'm honored that you've picked up this read. Here you will find love, adventure, and raw truth. It's my first of many—which details my unconventional love story with the Lord and how He redeemed my life from the pit. Yes--the pit of hell, but we'll get to that a little later.

Growing up as the youngest of the preacher's three kids, I've always struggled with perfectionism. For so many years I immersed my mind in the thought that "every piece of who I was had to ooze perfection." The perfect life, the perfect body, the perfect relationship, and the list goes on and on. This toxic mindset led me into the arms of a six-year ungodly relationship that quickly became an idol. Dancing to the tune of toxicity for so long nearly killed me, as I strived to be someone that the Father never created me to be.

After years of living in this facade, it took a towering toll on my mental—causing me to attempt to end my own life. Yes— the life

Abide. Arise. Ascend

that the Lord has given me that was never truly mine for the taking. I was lost, broken, and breathless. I was shameful, fractured, and bruised. Yet and still-- right there in the pit of my gruesome unraveling, the Father was right there to catch me at the bottom. As I began to experience the greatest love I've ever known, the depths of my heart started to fall madly in love with the one who rescued me.

This friend is my story and I'm elated to share it with you...

Journey with me.........................

Abide- Obey or act in accordance with

Arise- Come Forth or stand up

Ascend- Soar or fly

Abide. Arise. Ascend

Romans 6:12-13

"12 Let not sin therefore reign in your mortal body, that ye should obey it in the lusts thereof.

13 Neither yield ye your members as instruments of unrighteousness unto sin,"

Abide. Arise. Ascend

Part I

ABIDE.

Mastering Perfect Instability
True Life: I hate the girl in my mirror

Abide. Arise. Ascend

Romans 5:8

"8 But God demonstrates his own love for us in this: While we were still sinners, Christ died for us."

Abide. Arise. Ascend

My grandmother once told me about a movie called "Dr. Jekyll and Mr. Hyde." The storyline plot of the film is one of great chaos. It details the accounts of a man with split personalities struggling with everyday life. One of his personalities is known as "Mr. Jekyll," who longs to do good, while his other personality known as "Mr. Hyde," battles with internal evil.

While this lifestyle of split personalities is one that's been adopted by the culture for over a decade, the Bible states that a double-minded man is unstable in all his ways (James 1:8).

For years, I was someone who lived the double-minded life all too well. I was someone who'd learned to be perfectly religious but lacked a true foundational relationship with the Lord. Choosing to be defined by society rather than by Christ, I found my identity in so many fruitless things of this world. You know that girl who finds her validation, self-worth, and confidence in her outward appearance and the disease that social media can become? That was me.

The Beginning

Let's take it all the way back to Taylor Road Elementary School. This puts me around eight-years-old in the 4th grade. I was new to the school and only knew one girl who just so happened to be my cousin. At this stage in my 4th-grade life, I was pretty chunky. Hear me, I was beautiful but carried a little extra weight for my age. Being the youngest of the preacher's three kids, I was the baby of the family, yet I was the biggest in size. Although I was extremely loved and had an amazing family who knew the Lord, it was those small jokes people would make that helped diminish my confidence at an early age. You know the jokes that go, "hey chunky-butt." "You look like Freshie's big girl," and the list goes on and on. I was the younger sibling that would crack jokes,

Abide. Arise. Ascend

but the moment someone mentioned my weight-- joking or not, I couldn't take the heat.

Although I knew these jokes were intended to be all fun and games, I couldn't handle the weight of torment that would flood my heart when I was alone at night. With oozing insecurities, the opinions of others always had the capacity to cripple my heart. How could a person be so insecure? I was young, yes— and unaware of who I was made to be in Christ.

A Huge Shift

When I hit the 6th grade, I was finally allowed to get my hair flat ironed for the very first time by my Aunt Lisa. And although this may seem rather simplistic, in my world it was a huge game-changer! I was never allowed to get a perm or relaxer because I didn't need one. My hair is naturally curly but would normally be in long braids. But when I got my first silk press, I began to feel different. With black

Abide. Arise. Ascend

glistening strands of hair down my back, I began to feel prettier than I'd ever felt, and confidence began to exude out of me in a new way. I mean you couldn't tell sis anything, and yes-- sis is me.

Now in the 7th grade, I made the decision to start running track. Yes, me— one of the most uncoordinated people you'll ever meet. Since I had new hair followed by newfound confidence, I knew running track would slim me down in size. So the journey began, and after several months, everyone around me could see that my body was certainly changing. I finally seemed to be coming into the young girl I believed would make me happy to be.

Being young and naïve, this was the birthing of a monster of insecurities. As someone who never felt pretty enough, never felt skinny enough, and never felt beautiful...the moment my outward appearance began to change, so did I. I began to find validation in compliments, attention, and

Abide, Arise, Ascend

praise. I didn't know who I was, only who I thought I should be. Even with my newfound body, newfound confidence, and the new attention I wasn't used to receiving...I still wasn't happy.

I remember days where I'd sit and ponder on how I thought things would be different. "If I could just slim down...then life would get easier...then I'd know who I am. Right?" Wrong.

While I was trying to grow through my insecurities and didn't know much of who I was...if there was one thing I knew for sure, it was that I was going to be a journalist. Reporting the who, what, when, where, why, and how was my calling, and I knew it. So my freshman year of high school, I began to thrust myself into becoming just that, a journalist.

During my first year at Licking Heights High School, I became one of the head anchors for our "Broadcast Journalism," class. Through this course, we'd put together a weekly newscast that would be broadcast on every

Abide. Arise. Ascend

television in the building as the entire school watched. Doing this every week and having people affirm me with their words became addicting-- and the exact thing I didn't need.

Through this weekly routine, I had found what I viewed as a way of escape. I had begun to use journalism as a way to hide my internal insecurities. You know, the ones I was able to mask well but never truly dealt with. When I would get in front of that camera, it was as if nothing in life mattered but who people on the receiving end thought that I was. Yes, I was focused, determined, and driven, but I wasn't happy because I still didn't know "me." My lack of awareness of who Jordyn was drove me into the arms of a very unhealthy relationship. Over the course of five and a half years, that relationship quickly became my identity, my all, my God.

Abide. Arise. Ascend

Amour Eteral.
A love never intended to last forever.

I know you probably read this chapter title and thought to yourself..."Was this a misprint?" There is definitely an "N," in "eternal." While that is the correct spelling of the word, it was spelled intentionally without it. Why? I'm glad you asked.

On my left forearm, I have one of five tattoos that reads "amour eteral," which means "love eternal." This was a matching tattoo that I got with a boy who I was in a relationship with for 5 ½ years. "How could someone get a misspelled tattoo?" I know...and what makes it so bad was that I wrote it out for the tattoo artist and said it looked great when he asked me for my final approval. This permanent decision was rushed and not well thought out. All because I believed that if "ink" bonded us together, nothing could ever tear us apart. Well, friends...I later found that this love was truly never intended to last forever, so let's talk about it.

Questions? Answers??

What is forever? A long time? An eternity? A destination? What is love? A feeling? An emotion? A facade? How can we truly be in pursuit of something if we fail to grasp the root of what it is?

I remember being fifteen years old and getting into my first serious relationship, so I thought. "Babyface," that's what he used to call me; hopelessly devoted, it was young love at its finest. You know the kind of love that makes your heart skip a beat. The kind of love that is intoxicating in the worst way. The kind of love where you both stay on the phone all night long just so your call log would say you spoke for hours on end.

This was the kind of love where I'd risk telling my parents I was staying the night at a friend's house all so that I could actually stay the night with him. We were young, dumb, in

Abide. Arise. Ascend

love, and horny. At that age, every emotion feels so intense and deep, and I felt it all.

January 1, 2011, was the day our relationship became official. Back then, no relationship was ever solidified unless it was "Facebook official," so of course we made posts to make it known. While we were just two young kids, we both had so many broken pieces that needed healing. None of which either of us had the capacity to offer the other.

As a young girl who'd never been in something serious before, this relationship was a huge deal to me. Coming from a space of brokenness, I found validation in who I thought he wanted me to be. Even as a girlfriend, I vowed to give all of me and to do everything I could to make for a perfect relationship. The problem with this was that I didn't know who I was aside from my relationship status, and nothing or no one can ever be perfect, but God the Father!

Being in a space of feeling wanted and desired felt good in every way. For years I

Abide. Arise. Ascend

longed for his approval, affirmation, and love daily. It was a drug that I relied heavily on in the worst way. If he forgot to tell me I looked beautiful, I didn't feel like I was. If he didn't affirm the treasured value that I was, depression would meet me at my front door. I sought after these things in a boy who was incapable of meeting my internal needs. If he ever got upset with me, I felt like my world was caving in, and my heart would feel fractured. Every piece of who I was had become entangled in this "love eteral." I was at a place where I would do anything to make him happy. I'd spend money I didn't have, I would spend more time with him than I did my own family and my entire life was rooted in him.

Walking in Deception

Over the years, I began to develop very unhealthy behaviors and patterns from my lack of identity. While we were both so very young, we were invested in each other's lives mentally, physically, financially, and emotionally.

Abide. Arise. Ascend

Wrapped up in lust and wonder, I chose to be blinded by my flesh for the sake of what I thought I desired. At that moment, he was my everything, and I searched for hope in him; a hope that I later would come to realize can only be found in Christ Jesus.

"You shall have no other Gods before me." (Exodus 20:3)

For 5 ½ years, this boy had truly become an idol in my life. He became the only person I thought I needed. "Just you and me against the world," I used to say. Painfully, I learned that was not truly the case.

I remember the first time he cheated...yes cheated. I was horrified, angry, outraged, and broken. "You're just too good for me..." is what he'd always tell me like that was an excuse. Even so, it affected me. In those moments, I began to feel the weight of "not being good enough." I'd started to think that something was wrong with me, that I'd never

Abide. Arise. Ascend

be enough. "Maybe I'm crazy...maybe if I could just go from a size 4 to a size 0 then he'd stop this," I thought to myself. Or maybe if my butt was bigger than somehow he'd only have eyes for me.

After the first time, and the second time, and the third time, he'd always use his words to win my heart back all over again. He'd cash me out and buy me gifts and mentally manipulate my love for him. Although I knew him hurting me this way was wrong, somehow in my twisted mind, I'd believe his every word and take him back every single time. Why?

"Why would I take him back and believe him even when I'd have proof that he was lying?"

At the time for me, it was simple, he was all that I knew, he meant everything to me, and the thought of "starting over" wasn't something I was willing to stomach. I had made up my mind that no matter how bad things got

Abide. Arise. Ascend

between us, I'd always take him back so that I would never have to face being alone. Crazy right?

I remember most nights the mental manipulation and heartache would keep me awake. With a face full of tears and wide eyes, I would cyber-stalk these girls he'd messed around with as I compared myself to them. Can I keep it real? I was a wreck. Anytime I was alone, I was falling apart.

Hopelessly depressed, I would sink into the thought that "being cheated on was better than being alone..." I remember nights where I'd cry and drink myself to sleep as a way to medicate and numb my pain as a temporary fix. However, when it came to being out in public or even down to social media, you would never know how I was really doing. Why? From a young age, I had learned the art of "masking things well."

On my social media, I always projected this image of imminent perfection because, for years, that's how I wanted to be perceived. I

Abide. Arise. Ascend

was on Instagram giving advice about healthy relationships and value and self-worth when those weren't even things I was processing in my own life. That's both sad and grieving.

Since I had become so good at "saving face," oftentimes even my family and friends couldn't tell when I wasn't well. I could be in a room full of people projecting a joyous smile, but on the inside, my heart would be screaming! In those moments, I felt like I was suffocating in the middle of the street, but no one could see me dying. It wasn't because they didn't care that they didn't "see me," but simply because I refused to let them into my reality. I always felt like since I came from an amazing family that had such a rich history with the Lord, I had to suck it up and be strong all the time. So that is what I tried to do.

Drifting

In January of 2016, he landed a job with a police department in the "peach state." Was I excited for him? Of course! But honestly, I was

Abide. Arise. Ascend

devastated at the thought of him leaving and us having to be in a long-distance relationship. After investing well over four years of my life into this, I was not about to stand by and watch as the man I loved moved to another state. So what did I do? I did what "classic Jordyn," would do. I applied for and got an internship with CNN Atlanta to secure employment. I then packed my bags and moved to the A with him. Although my parents and family weren't in agreement with us living together unmarried, I didn't care. I was "in love," and "grown," so I thought-- and did it anyway.

So, there I was, all moved into our new place. Every day I was so excited to wake up next to him and to kiss him before bed every night. At the time, it felt so right. After all these years, we were finally living together, and I didn't have to sneak around anymore.

When I landed the internship at Turner Broadcasting (CNN HQ), I really began to think things were falling into place. Now that I had the perfect job and lived with my man, I

Abide. Arise. Ascend

thought living together was the solution to our problems.

"If we're living in the same house, he'd have no way to ever cheat on me again,"
I thought to myself.

Honestly, I used to think that my beauty could prevent him from messing around, or certainly my accomplishments could stop him from hurting me in the name of love, but no, that did not become the case.

With each month in the academy, I began to see a change in him. Not one for the better, but one for the worst. From his attitude to certain character traits; he was changing right before my eyes, and I felt as if the person I knew was fading...

Abide. Arise. Ascend

Thursday, November 24, 2016
Atlanta, Ga.

Thanksgiving Day in the beautiful state of Georgia! This of course is a national holiday, but this one for me would be bittersweet. Although I was happy to indulge in perfect fall weather with my boo, I was away from my family. Since both of our immediate families were back in our hometown, we spent the holiday with a bonus family that was sort of like family to us both. During dinner, we had a great time catching up with them and just being surrounded by people that we loved.

Towards the end of the night, I was getting tired and told my boo that I was going to head home and that I would see him there later. He leaned in and kissed me and walked me to my car. I remember, at that moment I felt loved, cared for, and safe. Until I got home...

Abide. Arise. Ascend

Breaking point

When I walked into our apartment, I got undressed, showered, and got comfortable. After my shower, something in me felt uneasy, causing me to desire to go looking through his things. When I opened his workbook bag, I saw his iPad, which I paid for every month, so in my mind, technically it belonged to me. At that moment I wavered between "why are you looking through his stuff?" and "you are going to find something if you crack the code on the iPad." So there I was...torn between two very different decisions. After thinking for a few seconds, I decided to go for it and began guessing possible passwords.

After a few attempts, I got it unlocked and thought to myself, "Oh God...there's no going back now." Once unlocked, I went to the photo section. In the "screenshots" album there was a screenshot of a text message between my then-boyfriend and one of his female co-workers. At the time, that co-worker was in a relationship with a woman she'd been with for years. In the message, she said, "I can't wait for Jordyn to go back to Ohio to visit your families so I can stay the night and be with you again..." As my eyes locked in on that screenshot and my head began to spin, I could feel my heartbeat echoing a million miles a minute, and I was breaking.

There as I stood alone, streams of tears began to rush down my face, and rage began to exude from the depths of my insides. "How could he do this to me? But she's gay, right? Am I really not good enough that this time he had to cheat on me with a girl that likes girls and dresses like a guy?" These are questions that began to invade my mind and sent me into a whirlwind of emotions. Full of hurt, anger, and rage, I got into my car and left.

"Now if there's anything that people know about me when I'm upset, I do not need my car keys. "

Abide. Arise. Ascend

Although I was upset and very uneasy, instead of doing something stupid, I pulled into a nearby Walmart parking lot to take a moment to grasp what was going on. I was so angry I couldn't breathe, see or speak. My body was shutting down and I needed help. So, I called "Officer D." I know you're probably wondering, "who's that?"

Earlier in the summer, I came across a woman on Instagram who was an Atlanta police officer and also a minister at a church. As someone who was raised in ministry, and at the time was new to being in a relationship with a police officer, I felt drawn to her. So, I reached out to her, and her kindness blew my mind. Throughout the summer we'd text, facetime, and spend time with one another. One of the things I was most grateful for when it came to her was that she seemed like an answered prayer. Not only was she looking to help me surrender my life to Christ, but she'd also help me to better understand my then-boyfriend when it came to certain situations

Abide. Arise. Ascend

with his career path since she too was an officer.

After getting to know her and developing true trust with her, I knew I could always count on her. So back to the Walmart parking lot, in that moment of complete catastrophe, I called her. After a few minutes of trying to catch my breath, I was finally able to explain what was going on.

At the time, she was on duty in Zone 6 and couldn't leave that area. For anyone who knows ATL, zone 6 is on the Eastside of Atlanta. I was in a city called "Lithonia," which is nearly 45 minutes away from her. Yet even in that moment from miles away, she was present and there to help me walk through my reality.

As the tears began to rush down my face, she began to speak life over me, she began to affirm the Love that Christ had for me and the daughter that I was in his eyes.

Abide. Arise. Ascend

"One of the many things I will forever be
grateful for regarding that moment
was that she saw me."

She saw through me being "the preacher's kid, the journalist and the girl people always thought was just so perfect." At that moment, even still living in sin, I could literally feel the love of the Father through her prayers, her covering, and protection.

When she finished praying, we talked for about an hour. Although I was still deeply hurt and broken, I felt calm enough to go home. So there I was; heading home to face the reality that I'd attempted to run from.

Reality Check

When I arrived home, I sat on the couch thinking about how this could happen to me, why I wasn't enough and how I'd let it get this far. Surely I was out of my mind to think this was love, right?

Abide. Arise. Ascend

While this cheating thing was nothing new under the sun, this time felt different because I couldn't take it anymore. No longer could I fathom the thought that every few months we'd be here again. Although Officer D. brought about a sense of peace while I talked with her, as my heart pondered on how bad my situation really seemed, it was almost like my heart became angry and full of rage all over again. At that moment I went and grabbed the iPad and sat on the island in the kitchen waiting for him to come home. There I sat, with a cup full of Hennessy in one hand and the iPad in the other.

About 20 minutes went by and he wasn't home. Then 30 minutes went by, and still no sight of him. After roughly an hour, he walks in with two of our male friends, and of course, they're drunk too. Immediately at the sight of him I threw the iPad at him and began going crazy. "How could you do this to me again? You're such a liar. Why do you think this is okay," I screamed at him. As I cried, yelled, and

Abide. Arise. Ascend

began to break, he tried to calm me down. At the same time, our friends began to tell me that whatever is on the iPad isn't real and that he'd never do me wrong. "He's the faithful friend..." they said.

As I continued to break into a million pieces, I tried to attack him. While he's 6'2 and I'm 5'2, my rage gave me the courage and strength to let him have it like never before. As I grew angrier and angrier I wouldn't stop trying to attack him. He picked me up and carried me into the bathroom and closed the door behind us. He then put me into the bathtub to restrain me, and no, there was no water inside of it. "Babe...you have to calm down," he told me. "I know this looks bad, but I did not actually cheat on you..." At that moment, I felt numb to no end. The proof was there on the iPad and yet and still my heart almost found a way to believe what my eyes had seen was simply a misunderstanding.

Abide. Arise. Ascend

Heading Home

When I finally calmed down, he let me go, and I went into our bedroom and cried for hours. That night when he and I went to bed, I was wide awake, trying to process every moment of our extensive young-love relationship. I thought to myself... "I can't get past this, not this time." So, the next morning I packed my life into my little car and prepared to go all the way back home to Ohio. But of course, not before we got into one last argument. At that moment, I never knew that would be the last time I would ever see him. Full of internal wounds and external emotional instability, I looked into his eyes for the last time and went home.

Abide. Arise. Ascend

iDIE.
Reporting LIVE from the ER

Sunday, December 4, 2016
Columbus, Ohio

"We're here, live tonight at a home on the Eastside of Columbus where a 21-year-old female has overdosed on prescription pills and alcohol. Neighbors tell us this was an attempted suicide and a desperate cry for help! We'll be sure to bring you the latest on how this story unfolds. Jordyn Dunlap for eye-witness news..."

This is how I remember it from my own lens...It was a super cold night on the evening of December, 4th, 2016. I had just arrived back from Atlanta the day prior. Coming home knowing that my 5 ½ year relationship was on the verge of being in shambles left me chaotic. I felt like my world was coming to an end, and I was desperate to cling to things that had already let me go.

Abide. Arise. Ascend

That night I decided I was going to go to the bar and get super drunk and then kill myself. Yes, straight like that. So, I reached out to a couple of friends from college who I knew where always down to have a good time. From there, we planned our night, met up, and made it happen.

As I sat in the car waiting for my friends to arrive, I called my ex and left him a voicemail saying something like this: "I literally hate that I love you. You are so undeserving of the love that I have to give, and after tonight, you will never hear from me again." Moments later, I was in the zone throwing back one shot after another, no chaser. Listening to the music that began to get me hyped, while the liquor seemed to eradicate the war that was going on inside my mind, I was drunk. I desired to drink until I couldn't feel a thing.

After a few hours of good music, good laughs, and lots of money on alcohol, we decided to go to another bar. When we got there, I remember getting out of the car feeling

Abide. Arise. Ascend

like I couldn't feel my face. My vision began to blur, and suddenly I didn't want to go inside the second bar anymore. Yet and still, I clung onto one of the two friends with me and made it inside. For about an hour, we danced, ridiculously then decided to leave.

Now while I was super drunk and seemed to be "enjoying myself," my mental plan of killing myself was still very present in my mind. Being the youngest of the preacher's three kids, if there was one thing I knew, it was that I could never walk into my parents' home intoxicated. That wasn't a thing. So, I decided to stay over at my friend's house since we were already together.

The next morning I woke up still super drunk, hung-over, and depressed, but I wanted to go home. I checked in with my friends and let them know I was getting ready to head out. As I drove home, all I could think about was how crappy my life felt at that moment. The weight of my depression was hitting me harder than usual, and my heart was so heavy.

Abide. Arise. Ascend

After about 10 minutes, I arrived at my parent's home and just sat in my car. I knew they'd be at church so I would be alone. There I sat as my mind was racing a mile a minute and I couldn't turn it off. "How could you let this happen to you, Jordyn?" "You really let this n**** get away with cheating on you again?" "You deserve to die for how stupid you are!" These are just a few of the demonic lies that began to make their home in my heart.

As I sat there, I honestly thought myself into a deeper level of depression by the minute. I thought about the years I invested my time, my heart, my money, my body, and my life into this relationship. I pondered the work, the blood, the sweat, and the tears I'd invested into making this boy right for me, and the thought of someone tampering with that made me crazy in the brain! At that moment,

"I honestly felt that I'd rather die than to be without the person who continues to abuse my love."

Abide. Arise. Ascend

The more he pushed me away for things that he'd done wrong, the more I was desperate to hold onto him. Wild, right?

The Choice Between Life & Death

After an hour of contemplating if my life was even worth living anymore, I agreed with the devil and decided that I was going to kill myself right there, in my car. I walked into my parent's home and rushed into their bathroom in search of pills. Now, my father had a slipped disk in his vertebrae, so I knew there were prescription pills in the house.

In an effort to take my own life, I grabbed every pill bottle I saw and walked back out to my car. Desperate to feel anything while trying to cope with years of trauma alone, I was ready to "make the pain go away." I was ready to feel numb to the chaos going on inside of me, but if I'm honest...at first, I couldn't do it. I sat there and sat there and sat there before I was finally ready to comprehend what I was about to do. It was time, 5 minutes later, I started swallowing prescription pills by the mouth-full. I started with 10, 20, 30, 40...until I got to 43. Yep! My drunken butt was counting. When I was done all I could do was cry.

Hopeless, I sat there waiting for my insides to erode. After my tears began to slowly drift, I remember falling into a deep sleep. Hours passed and my parents were just arriving home from church to see my car parked in their driveway. While they weren't expecting me, I was sitting in the driver's seat of my car when they got there. Not on my phone, or eating or reading a book... but unresponsive, unconscious, and overdosed. I know what you're probably thinking, 'Not the preacher's kid? Not the journalist?' but yes. This is my truth, and it's raw. I'd probably been there in that physical state for about 2 hours before them finding me.

For all of the parents out there...can you imagine finding your baby girl this way? Imagine this...They walk up to my window and

Abide. Arise. Ascend

my mom says, "babe, what are you doing here? Come inside." She said, originally she thought I'd just fallen asleep...until she opened my car door and I fell out into her arms. As she caught me, her eyes caught the attention of dozens of pills plastered all over my lap as well as on the floor of my car. These were the ones that didn't make it to my bloodstream.

"Quick...we've got to get her to a hospital...Joe, hurry," she said to my father. Second, after second you could hear the heartbeats of my parents echoing outside of their bodies. It was as if time was standing still— yet slowly caving in. I remember fading in and out of consciousness. I remember being held in the backseat while teardrops of devastation fell onto my forehead from my mother's face.

"The cries of my father, the urgency in my mother's voice to drive faster, the very little breath I still had left in my lungs. I was dying, and if I'm

Abide. Arise. Ascend

honest, I knew I was on a one-way ticket headed straight to hell."

As we drove, I remember seeing the beams of traffic lights then being rushed into the emergency room right before blacking out. The next time my eyes were opened, I felt like an amnesiac. The very moment I saw light, I began to panic. "Why am I handcuffed to this bed? What are all of you doing here? Why am I here..." I screamed! I can remember my aunt Lisa and my grandmother talking to me. I remember having to be escorted to the bathroom and not being able to do anything alone. I remember my brother being extremely upset and the worry in my mother's eyes that pierced my heart. "What have I done...?" I thought to myself. At that moment, I knew my life would never be the same. Not only had I overdosed on more than 30 prescription pills that didn't belong to me, but now I've hurt the people that I love.

In the ER I was given a cup of melted charcoal to drink. Their hope was that this

Abide. Arise. Ascend

disgusting concoction would cause my body to throw up everything I had just ingested. Although with every gulp I thought I was going to pass out, it actually worked. The poison I had put into my body was coming out, and now I had to deal with my present reality. The night before I went to the bar with the intention of getting drunk and crashing my truck to end my life. I just didn't have the grit to go through with it. I didn't care who my car wrecked, who it would affect, or who'd be caught in the crossfire. I just knew I couldn't handle the weight of my reality any longer, so I viewed death as an escape, but I was still here....

So let's backtrack...before going to the bar the night before, I went to my brother's house and talked to my sister-in-law. Overwhelmed with my relationship problems, I'd expressed how I just couldn't take it anymore. "I'm fine. I just need to walk away this time..." I told her. After wiping my eyes and pulling myself together, I carried my newborn niece Harmony into the bathroom

Abide. Arise. Ascend

with me to take a bunch of "mirror pics." At just five months old, she smiled and entertained our mini photoshoot.

"You're so beautiful, and no matter what, I want you to always remember me..." I said to her. That night, I told my sweet little Harmony that I'd never see her again and cried as I held her because I actually believed that."

I believed that she'd grow up not knowing me, and all I'd be to her was a mere memory.

Fast forward back to the emergency room...So the next morning when I woke up, my parents were sitting with me. My mother looks at me and says, "your father and I have talked it through, and we think it's best to send you someplace where you can receive the help that you need." In an instant, my blood began to boil, my heart began to pound, and it was almost as if the room was spinning, but I couldn't move. "Wow..." I thought to myself. "I really messed up big time."

A few hours later, my nurses came into my room and prepared me to be transported to a mental health hospital. "We'll meet you there babe. We'll be following right behind you," my mom told me. I remember riding in the ambulance on the way to Dublin Springs Mental Health Hospital where I stayed. All I could think about was how I was really in over my head this time. I was broken, I felt so lonely and I couldn't believe I reached this low of a breaking point. The drive felt extensive. Mile after mile, it felt like we'd been driving for an eternity long. Finally, we came to a complete stop. The door opened, and I was being wheeled out.

As promised, my parents were right by my side. Now prior to coming to Dublin Springs, I spent three days on suicide watch in the hospital. Every night my mother stayed with me, but she would not be able to this time.

Abide. Arise. Ascend

When we arrived at the hospital, they took us back into this private room. Now originally, my parents told me I'd just be here overnight. "Since you'll be admitted here for the week, we'll need to get a quick photo and confiscate any devices you may have," the nurse said. Instantly, I broke down in tears as she took the photo that felt more like a mug shot. "I'm sorry okay! I didn't mean to do this. Please don't leave me here. Please!" I shouted to my parents that were just feet away from me. It seemed as if my whole world was diminishing right before my very eyes and there wasn't a thing I could do to cling to it.

Facing Reality

After my parents got me to calm down a little and reassured me this was for my good, I hugged them and was taken on the journey that I'll never forget. My first night in the psych ward was by far the toughest. Just moments after my parents left, I was taken to my new room and an older male was screaming, talking to himself, and threw a chair. Before taking another step, I broke down in fear and asked the nurse if I could have a phone call. Sobbing hysterically... "Mom, please come get me! I can't stay here. I'm begging you! Please come get me," I said. As I was talking to my mom, I could hear my father in the background whaling in tears. The only time I'd ever seen my father cry was at my grandmother's funeral. That night will go down in history as one of the toughest days of my life.   I was a wretched mess, and my mess seemed to be affecting every person proximal to me.

At the end of that phone call, my parents prayed with me and affirmed their love for me. The next day when my family came to visit, I was even worse. I was emotionally unstable and my mind was still so diluted. Although I was so grateful to see my loved ones, I was so embarrassed for them to see me in that space. I remember telling my sister-in-law, "I have to get out of here...I have to go to Atlanta to host an event this weekend." Little did I understand

I wasn't in a healthy enough space to go anywhere other than where I was.

While it was bad enough that I was dealing with what I had done, I was even more hurt that after being hospitalized for a suicide attempt, my boyfriend of 5 ½ years that I'd given everything to didn't even come to see me, didn't call, nothing at all.

Although my mind was still focused on what put me in the place where I was, my plan for healing and recovery was in process. During my stay, I was placed on an antidepressant called Lexapro and saw a psychiatrist daily. Every day, there would be different group activities, lunch, and ways to connect with people. During those times of "connecting," I remained alone in my room, disconnected, still trying to process it all.

Abide. Arise. Ascend

Facing the Truth

In the coming days— I was in for the biggest reality check of my life. I remember sitting in the "entertainment" lounge with my roommate braiding her hair and she said to me, "you know you're never going to get out of here if you continue to seclude yourself, right?"
Was that right? Was staying to myself doing me more harm than good? I mean, was I making the wrong decision again? Known as the "Journalist," or the "preacher's kid," it was there in the psychiatric ward where titles didn't mean a thing, and I still couldn't believe I was there.

One night, one of the nurses came to me and said, "Hi pretty...what are you here for?" Full of anxiety, I told her I was there because I attempted suicide. Instantly, she smiled and said, "Wow...yeah, you don't belong here baby girl. I could see that the moment I laid eyes on you. God is going to get you through this, and you're going to go home." Right there at that moment, I broke down. It was as if God himself

Abide. Arise. Ascend

dispatched his angels to guard and protect me, just as it says in Psalm 91:11.

For he will command his angels concerning you to guard you in all your ways;

On my third night I was in the shower washing my hair and completely fell apart. As the water fell on every part of me, I was a wreck, but the Lord was present. I remember crying out, "God!!!!! I don't even know where to go, what to say or how to move, but I need you.

"I need you to heal my broken heart and to show me your love once more."

No matter how hard this may become if you get me through this...whatever you say, I'll do."

This was my life-changing moment of coming to the end of myself. It was the beginning of a life I never thought I'd live to

Abide. Arise. Ascend

see. Right there in the shower at a psychiatric hospital, the Lord began to answer my prayer as I started to encounter the man Christ Jesus. It was almost like in an instant he began to dismantle my very broken heart that had rooted itself in hopelessness. Right there at that moment, he began to cleanse me with his love and fill me afresh with his spirit. Oh, how grateful I felt, oh how hopeful my heart became there alone with him.

There was no music, no one laying their hands on me, but the Lord our God. In that moment, I knew the Lord responded to my desperation. The hunger inside of me that longed for him was met by his love. The wild thing is that he placed the desire in me to even desire him!

A New Perspective

After this encounter with the Lord, I got up, turned the water off, and looked in the mirror. When the fog on the glass cleared and I saw myself...I began to weep even more

Abide. Arise. Ascend

uncontrollably. "You're going to make it through this, and you're so much more than where you are right now," I told myself. Although I was still in the psychiatric hospital, the next morning I woke up with so much joy in my heart. For the first time in a long time, I had encountered Jesus in a way that I knew would change my life. Although I didn't know how or what that would look like, I was hopeful.

Throughout the next day, I felt different, walking around with a heart full of expectancy and wonder of all that God would do through me. The joy I felt was fueled by each family visit. When they came to visit, it was never with sappy wet eyes, but with joy that I needed to feel from them. They were filled with so much love, kindness, and compassion and continued to love me beyond the reality of where I was at that moment.

My tribe is one of the most pivotal reasons that I'm alive today and growing into the woman they've known all along that I

Abide. Arise. Ascend

would be. They were also one of the key factors in me truly submitting my life to Christ, but we'll get to that a little later.

After a very long seven days, the day finally came where I'd be released from the hospital. While I had waited for this day and longed to go home, part of me was nervous.

As the afternoon came, my things were packed and ready to go. When the time came, I was met by the gentle embrace of my father, eager to get me home. As we walked closer and closer to the entrance, I couldn't believe it. I had received a second chance at life and I wasn't going to waste this one.

The moment the fresh air hit my face, all I could do was smile from ear to ear. This was the first time in a long time that I'd tasted and seen that God was good.

When we left the hospital, we went to breakfast, and I remember my dad handing me my cell phone. Before I even turned it on, I looked at it full of nerves and thought about the kinds of messages that would be inside. I

Abide. Arise. Ascend

thought about everything that had happened in a week, and I was ready to rejoin the world.

The major thing I was looking forward to most was becoming a version of me that I never knew. I was committed to no longer living a broken life at a distance from the Lord, and so although I knew I had a long way to go, I was ready for that journey of becoming me.

Abide. Arise. Ascend

Malachi 3:7

"Return unto me, and I will return unto you, saith the LORD"

Part II

ARISE.

iLIVE

Learning to walk again

Abide. Arise. Ascend

"One of the hardest things was learning that I was worth recovery..."

– Demi Lovato.

*W*hile being released from the psychiatric hospital came with a great deal of joy, it also came with an abundance of inner work that I needed to unpack. Yes, it was time to get down to the nitty-gritty. It was time to heal in real-time and do the work I'd been saying I'd do all along in order for me to leave the psych ward.

When choosing to recover, one of my first orders of business was getting home and getting to know myself for real, for the first time. Learning what "Jordyn," likes, and dislikes? What makes my heart come alive? What moves me and what rattles me to my core.

The journey of discovering me was not an easy path. I spent a lot of sober nights alone, undone, and unraveled. Sometimes nights were filled with tears of grief and others were filled with an abundance of joy. Dear friends, this part of my journey is called "recovery."

Abide. Arise. Ascend

During my healing process, one of the most pivotal things that helped to benefit me was committing to therapy. I know what you're probably thinking..." you see a shrink?" I sure did and I still do. I've been seeing a therapist since December of 2016, and while at the time I didn't know how much of a healing balm it would be for me, it has been extremely beneficial. Let's rewind though as I tell you about my first day in counseling.

The Birth of Healing

Picture this...a young woman fresh out of the psych ward, struggling to find her truest identity, all the while still trying to heal from the internal wounds that punctured. I was a wreck, I was still unhappy and while I was on the road to healing, I was not yet whole.

Prior to my mental health journey, my perspective of therapy and those with mental health issues honestly was very limited to things I'd seen on television growing up. When I heard the words "mental illness" I associated them with people who displayed irate or outlandish behaviors. In my eyes "therapy," was when you sat on the couch of a stranger and poured your heart out as they told you what to do with all of your problems. Well friends...when I started my journey with therapy, my assumed perspective began to shift.

A Little backstory

My therapist is a woman of color who is saved and spirit-filled. Although I too am a believer, she has never forced her religious views onto me. In my first session, I remember being so angry and embarrassed about being there. "Why don't you tell me a little bit about yourself," she said politely. My response to her gentle gesture was rude and non-interested. "Um...can't you just read the paper that explains why I'm here?" I said back to her. While this therapist had done nothing wrong, I still carried a bit of residue from the world and had not yet surrendered my life to Christ.

Abide. Arise. Ascend

From the very first session, through my anger and frustration, she began to work with me and to help me break down walls and barriers that were preventing me from truly healing. One session turned into two sessions; two sessions turned into three, four, and more. Before I knew it, months had gone by, and I was actually beginning to benefit from going.

During those sessions, things weren't all glitz and glam. There were days when we began to unpack my childhood insecurities, which led to some of my adolescent decisions. In those moments of reality settling in, emotionally, I began to shatter into a million pieces. Right there in the climax of the breaking, she was there to help pray me through and to assist me in steering my process of navigating self.

For me, healing was gruesome. It was gritty and real. I was forced to confront internal scars that had bled for years, all because my pride convinced me that I was all good, all the time. During the peak of my healing process, I began to see God dismantle that classic lie.

Healing in Layers

Anyone who has gone through the healing process knows that there are multiple pieces to the process. For me, another major aspect of my healing has been my community. Their support has been a strong piece of my journey, even when I was unsure. To be honest, when I first set out on this journey, I didn't know what I needed from my community. I didn't know how I wanted or needed to be supported, so that alone was a journey of getting to. Yet and still, in my lack of truly knowing self, they loved me through my journey.

Another step of my process towards healing took me back to a campus ministry that was filled with young people like me that attended the church that I went to. These weren't your average young people, but ones that were hopelessly devoted to the Lord in such a rich way. Seeing them worship and love on Jesus the way that they did, made me excited and provoked me to pursue him deeper.

With this part of my community, we would have all-night prayer meetings, worship until our lungs gave out, and truly rest in his presence. I was being healed!

So, I kept showing up and committing to my journey, and after a while, it started paying off. I started to encounter Jesus in a new way; at home, in my car, and everywhere that I went. No matter where I went, the Lord began to exude worship out of me, just as David let out raw praises in the Psalms.

When I think about my healing journey, I'm reminded of the parable of the woman with the issue of blood. As mentioned in Matthew 9:20-22, Mark 5:25-34, and Luke 8:43-48. For those who aren't too familiar with her story, there was a woman who had been bleeding with a chronic illness for many years. Over those years, she'd seen countless doctors, seeking the best help she could find, but nothing seemed to be true healing for her. On the contrary, she actually became worse.

After years of spending her time, energy, and money on what seemed to be fruitless outlets of healing, she heard that Jesus was near. Although she'd never met him, she'd heard of the miracles that people would testify about regarding him and allowed her faith to become activated. So here she was, this woman who people would view as "dirty or unworthy," in need of a touch from the Lord.

She went to where she knew he'd be and reached out to touch the hymn of his garment. Mark 5:28-29 says, "*For she said if I can just touch his clothes I will be made well. Instantly her blood flow ceases, and she sensed in her body that she was healed from her affliction.*"

The text goes on, and Jesus questions who touched him because he'd felt power leave his body. Trembling before him, she falls at his feet and he says, *"Daughter, go in peace and be healed of your affliction..."* Whew Lord.

Abide. Arise. Ascend

Can you imagine? Here was this broken woman who searched for healing in so many different ways but still came up short every time. Based on something she heard about Jesus and the healing that he offered, she allowed her faith to lead her into his presence. Once she arrived in a space where she could be exposed to true healing, she stepped out with a heart of expectancy, and Jesus met her there. That's such a gift!

You see, it's not about how many years we've bled or how long we've been in a toxic relationship, but the question becomes, "What are we willing to do to encounter Jesus?" For me, that looked like letting go of anyone and anything that was no longer conducive to where I desired to go spiritually. It looked like learning to say no without an explanation and finally learning to show up for myself more than I did for others. It was through a love-sick, life-changing encounter with Jesus, spending time with my family, and committing to therapy that really helped to strengthen me.

Abide. Arise. Ascend

Through therapy and learning to receive the love of Christ for myself, I began to really know the Lord for Jordyn. Beyond other's testimonies, other's experiences, and other's encounters, I began to KNOW the Father for who He was to me.

After a few months, I remember talking to my campus pastor about baptism and telling him that I was ready to surrender my life. We met again and talked about the severity of it, and I was ready and set a date.

Hopelessly devoted
To the one whom my soul loves

Cues Smokey Norful, "Falling in love with Jesus. Falling in love with Jesus. Falling in love with Jesus is the best thing I've ever done."

On May 21, 2017, I surrendered my life to Christ. I was baptized in Jesus' name at Hope City House of Prayer by my older brother Josiah, and I've never been the same. My baptism was such a moment of awakening

Abide. Arise. Ascend

where the Lord showered me with his goodness. It was the moment of being taken down in Jesus name, knowing that I'd be cleansed of my shame, my guilt, my hurt, my sins, and the chaos that for so long was everything to me. It was there in that water grave that God set me on the path that changed my life forever! The path to FREEDOM!

Abide. Arise. Ascend

Psalms 27:4

"One thing have I desired of the LORD, that will I seek after; that I may dwell in the house of the LORD all the days of my life, to behold the beauty of the LORD, and to enquire in his temple."

Part III

ASCEND.

Taking flight;
The point of no return

Abide. Arise. Ascend

After my baptism, it seemed like my life began to really take off. While things were certainly not perfect, doing life with the Lord was my truest heart's desire. Through making that public declaration of surrender, I was sold on living for the man Christ Jesus.

Shortly after committing my life to Christ, he allowed me to start iLIVE The Movement, which is a mental health non-profit birthed through my testimony. Through events and providing different services, iLIVE serves as a platform of support for survivors of various forms of mental illness. Since birthing this ministry shortly after my baptism, the Lord has taken me to speaking engagements all across the country, from The Ohio State University to Howard University, from Eastern Michigan University to Ohio University in Athens. This platform has allotted me opportunities to share the Lord's testimony in rooms that I never dreamed or imagined I'd find myself in.

Abide. Arise. Ascend

I can remember countless times where I was speaking to someone and all I could think was, "wow...this is what it was all about." In moments of embracing broken young women who were on the verge of falling apart, I was honored to embrace every piece of them as they unraveled.

Creating this safe space was also very healing for me because I knew there were so many people out there who were going through what I had recently come out of. My desire was for them to see hope through experiencing the love of Christ in his presence.

Witnessing how radically the Lord changed my life intensified my desire for others to experience that same type of conversion. Once He truly got ahold of my heart, he began to change my desires, my perspective, and my entire life. The further I grew in love with Him, the more He began to shape and mold me. He gave me a heart for intercession and planted me in the house of prayer to raise up day and night worship through the rhythm of my life.

Abide. Arise. Ascend

"One of my biggest prayers, since I surrendered my life to Christ has been, "Lord, let my life lead people to your feet. When people look at me and the new life that you've given me, all I want them to see is you."

A Love Like No Other

You see, one of the greatest things that I love about Jesus is that He gives us the choice to receive him. Nothing is forced, and he always finishes what he starts. I think oftentimes we think the Lord is after our perfection when he's really just after our hearts.

You see, this paradigm of mind that says you have to 'get yourself together' before you pursue a relationship with Christ is a lie. We ourselves are not that powerful, but the true change from the inside out can only come from the Lord. When he hung his head and died, we were the joy set before him. He's the all-knowing God who is never surprised by our uncertainties or our shortcoming.

Since we were handcrafted by the Father himself, he knows our frame, our thoughts, our hearts, and our wills. Yet and still, he loves us even when we hurt his heart. When I laid down my life for Christ it didn't mean that I didn't still have to "do the work." It meant that even through those hurdles in life that would come; I'd be rooted in knowing who holds tomorrow.

This friends is called "soaring..." and the same God that brought me out of a life of dysfunction is the same God who longs to bring peace to your soul as well. He's faithful until the very end, and there is hope for where you are. You are greatly loved!

To the families that have unsaved family and friends that you're contending for; don't stop interceding on their behalf. Even if you don't see an immediate change in your projected timeline, just remember that the true way is in the Spirit, just as Ephesians 6:12 tells us.

Abide. Arise. Ascend

"For we wrestle not against flesh and blood, but against principalities, against powers, against the rulers of the darkness of this world, against spiritual wickedness in high places."

I had a feeling you'd be looking for more, so here's a story of encouragement...

Abide. Arise. Ascend

Shortly after surrendering my life to Christ, I found out that the same girl that my ex-boyfriend had been messing around with was now pregnant with his baby. Although I was saved and was coming into an identity I'd always longed for, I was still a bit hurt by this. Honestly, I was unsettled.

When I found out this news only about a year and some change had gone by. Even though Jesus was the newfound love of my life, I still had wounds that were in the process of healing.

One of the reasons this was such a hard pill to swallow was because he was having a baby with her, but he stood by as I aborted mine a while back. Yes, years ago, I stood in the bathroom waiting to see a test read "not pregnant," but it actually read the opposite. Being me, I took several tests, and they all read the same thing: pregnant!

At that time in my life, I was so selfish and viewed a "baby" as a liability, and chose not to keep it. While my then-boyfriend didn't

Abide. Arise. Ascend

force me to make that decision, he also didn't fight to keep the life either. That was beyond hurtful, traumatizing, and one of the most painful times in my life. The aftermath came with a lot of shame, guilt, anxiety, and depression that I had to submit to the Lord as I gave my life to him.

After hearing the news, I remember being at my pastor's sister's house and just trying not to break down. You see, over time, I had finally gotten to a space where I no longer viewed my story from the lens of victimization, but rather from the lens that we are all sons and daughters.

Months prior, the Lord had even led me to write my ex a letter affirming that I've forgiven him even for the things he's never apologized for. I apologized for the various mistakes I'd made while in the relationship as well. To see how everything played out; the cheating, leading me to attempt to kill myself, becoming hospitalized, and us never speaking again. Then he ends up having a child with the

Abide. Arise. Ascend

same girl that he told me not to worry about; it was a lot to process.

In spite of all these things, I'd already vowed to the Lord that no matter what, I'd never walk away from him. Right there in the pain that consumed me, I made the choice to lean into my community.

Through this, my sister in law Taylor and my friend India were right by my side. I didn't get through this hurtful situation because I'm "so strong" or "someone special," but simply because I didn't do it in my own strength. I allowed the Father to carry me. Through my weakness, his strength was made perfect. It was at that moment when I was reminded that I'm still in process. It was at that moment when I was reminded that until I'm caught up with him I'll always be growing, changing, and evolving into who he's called me to be.

In the process of life, we are allowed to grow, we are allowed to shift and we are allowed to learn in the process. Life is always

Abide. Arise. Ascend

going to be happening—to you, to me, to us. But no matter what, we get to do it with Jesus, and that's such a great reward!

I say this to say that no matter what this life may bring, come hell or high water, we serve a God that is able to do exceeding, abundantly above all that we could ever ask or think just as it says in Ephesians 3:20.

I challenge you in this moment if you are afraid to leave that relationship; you feel like you can never start that business, you don't know if you could ever heal from that childhood trauma, friend, I urge you to try Jesus. More than a judge, a ruler, and the holy one, he is a father, a friend, and the only way! His love for you is infinite, and I pray that in your darkest hours you will run to him. That his presence would be your home and that you'd come into relationship with him. There is nothing our God cannot do! After all, I'm still here standing tall, healed, and surrendered. Take his hand, he is waiting. Selah.

Abide. Arise. Ascend

Hey you!

Although my story was honest, genuine, and raw, I also know that it can be quite heavy to digest. For some, you may see yourselves, hear your own words, or even see a familiar path. If that is the case, I encourage you to lay it down! Pick up joy! Allow hope to fill your heart! You can make it! Know that Jesus is faithful, forever!

Love Jordyn

Abide. Arise. Ascend

Stay Connected with me on social media

iamjordyndunlap.org

 iamjordyndunlap

iamjordyndunlap_

Jordyn Dunlap

Jordynmdunlap

Abide. Arise. Ascend

Special thank you to my family and friends who supported me through one of the lowest moments of my life. Without you, I wouldn't be here today. I love you deeply, now, forever, and always.

Mom and Dad
Josiah and Taylor
Justina and Josh
Grandma Crockett
Shayanna Crone
Makeyah Croom
Robert Ryan Reid
Yaves Ellis
Kacia Grant
Aunt Tasha and Uncle Aaron
Tatiana Jordan
Uncle Wesley Dunlap
Aunt Lisa and Uncle Dane

Abide. Arise. Ascend

In every season of my life, it has been the word of the Lord that has brought healing, clarity, and joy to every piece of me. Even in moments of extreme chaos, when the culture would say I should be "losing my mind..." it's been in praying the scriptures that I've been able to see the hand of the Lord move just as he said that he would.

Here are some, but certainly not all, of the biblical truths that have continued to change my life. May they empower you to love, grow, and heal in the hands of your father, the man Christ Jesus.

Philippians 4:6-7
Be anxious for nothing, but in everything by prayer and supplication with thanksgiving let your requests be made known to God. And the peace of God, which surpasses all comprehension, will guard your hearts and your minds in Christ Jesus.

1 Peter 5:7
Casting all your anxiety on Him, because He cares for you.

Abide. Arise. Ascend

John 14:27
Peace I leave with you; My peace I give to you;
not as the world gives do I give to you. Do not
let your heart be troubled, nor let it be fearful.

Jonah 2:5-7
"Water encompassed me to the point of death.
The great deep engulfed me,
Weeds were wrapped around my head.
"I descended to the roots of the mountains.
The earth with its bars was around me forever,
But You have brought up my life from the pit, O
Lord my God.
"While I was fainting away,
I remembered the Lord,
And my prayer came to You,
Into Your holy temple.

Philippians 4:13
I can do all things through Him who
strengthens me.

2 Timothy 1:7
For God has not given us a spirit of timidity
(fear), but of power and love and discipline.

Isaiah 41:10
'Do not fear, for I am with you;

Abide. Arise. Ascend

Do not anxiously look about you, for I am your God.

I will strengthen you, surely I will help you, Surely I will uphold you with My righteous right hand.'

Matthew 11:28-30
"Come to Me, all who are weary and heavy-laden, and I will give you rest. Take my yoke upon you and learn from Me, for I am gentle and humble in heart, and you will find rest for your souls. For My yoke is easy and My burden is light."

Romans 8:6
For the mindset on the flesh is death, but the mindset on the Spirit is life and peace,

Source: https://bible.knowing-jesus.com/topics/Mental-Health

Abide. Arise. Ascend

Journal

_____

_____

_____

_____

_____

_____

_____

_____

_____

_____

_____

_____

_____

_____

_____

_____

_____

_____

_____

_____

_____

Journal

_____

_____

_____

_____

_____

_____

_____

_____

_____

_____

_____

_____

_____

_____

_____

_____

_____

_____

Journal

Journal

_____

_____

_____

_____

_____

_____

_____

_____

_____

_____

_____

_____

_____

_____

_____

_____

_____

_____

_____

_____

Abide. Arise. Ascend

Journal

Abide. Arise. Ascend

Journal

Abide. Arise. Ascend

Journal

Abide. Arise. Ascend

Journal

_____

_____

_____

_____

_____

_____

_____

_____

_____

_____

_____

_____

_____

_____

_____

_____

_____

_____

_____

_____

_____

_____

Abide. Arise. Ascend

Journal

Abide. Arise. Ascend

Journal

_____

_____

_____

_____

_____

_____

_____

_____

_____

_____

_____

_____

_____

_____

_____

_____

_____

_____

_____

_____

Abide. Arise. Ascend

Made in the USA
Monee, IL
16 September 2022

14091137R00060